D1244511

Cover illustration: A number of feature films using genuine Fokker fighters were produced between the wars, including *Hell's Angels* (1928), *DIII 88* (1938) and *Pour Le Mérite* (1938). The bulk of the triplane flying in both the 1938 films was carried out by Willy Gabriel, a wartime pilot with eleven confirmed victories who had served in *Jagdstaffel 11*. In this still from *Pour Le Mérite* he is flying the Clerget-powered Dr1 528/17.

VINTAGE WARBIRDS No 6

FOKKER FIGHTERS
of World War One

ALEX IMRIE

ARMS AND ARMOUR PRESS

Introduction

Published in 1986 by Arms & Armour Press Ltd.,
2–6 Hampstead High Street, London NW3 1QQ.

Distributed in the United States by Sterling
Publishing Co. Inc., 2 Park Avenue, New York,
N.Y. 10016.

© Arms & Armour Press Ltd., 1986
All rights reserved. No part of this publication may
be reproduced, stored in a retrieval system, or
transmitted in any form by any means electrical,
mechanical or otherwise, without first seeking the
written permission of the copyright owner.

British Library Cataloguing in Publication Data:
Imrie, Alex
Fokker fighters of World War One. –
(Vintage warbirds illustrated; 6)
1. Fokker airplanes – History
I. Title   II. Series
623.74'64   TL686.F6

ISBN 0-85368-782-X

Editing, design and artwork by Roger Chesneau.
Typesetting by Typesetters (Birmingham) Ltd.
Printed and bound in Italy by GEA/GEP in
association with Keats European Ltd., London.

◀2

1. (Title spread) One of the few units to be equipped
with the Fokker DVI was *Jagdstaffel 80b*, based at
Morsberg aerodrome in Elsass: six such aircraft are
seen here in August 1918. The unit had little success
with this machine, mainly because of lubrication
difficulties which resulted in many engine failures.
Pilots spoke highly of the aircraft's handling
qualities, however, and had it been re-fitted with a
more powerful and more reliable engine the type
might have made a name for itself.
2. One chore that befell the Fokker DV was
transition training: in order to familiarize stationary-
engine pilots with the different handling aspects of
aircraft powered by rotary engines, many fighting
units received a small number of these machines.
Twenty-five are recorded as being at the Front,
presumably being used in this capacity, at the end of
February 1918, mostly assigned to Albatros units in
the process of being re-equipped with Fokker DrI
triplanes. Making a practice flight for this purpose on
11 November 1917, *Leutnant* Tüxen of *Jagdstaffel 6*
lost control in a steep turn over Marckebeeke aerodrome and became entangled in the branches of a
tree, fortunately without injury. Note the hay wagons
to cushion the fall during retrieval!

Anthony Herman Gerard Fokker was born at Kediri in Java on 6
April 1890, the son of a Dutch coffee planter. Attracted to aviation, he
went to Germany in 1910, became involved in aircraft construction
and taught himself to fly on the second version of his Spider
monoplane, successfully taking the tests for his FAI Aviator's
Certificate (Germany Number 88) on 16 May 1911. Less than one year
later he had established his Fokker Aeroplanbau at Johannisthal near
Berlin, developing the Spider design and running a flourishing flying
school which attracted military students and soon began to supply
aeroplanes to the German Army.

Favourable conditions offered by the authorities caused Fokker to
move his production facilities to Schwerin-Gorries in Mecklenburg
towards the end of 1913, where the Fokker Flugzeugwerke GmbH
was to remain until the end of the First World War. His name first
came to the public's attention through his daring and skilful aerobatic
flying at Johannisthal before the war, and it became etched in history
when his machine-gun-armed monoplanes created heroes out of Max
Immelmann and Oswald Boelcke and caused the unwieldy BE
biplanes of the Royal Flying Corps to be referred to as 'Fokker
fodder'. It was highlighted again in 1918 when Allied airmen tended
to name all German fighting aeroplanes 'Fokkers'. From the earliest
days of the war Fokker established a rapport with the front-line
airmen: he was always willing to listen to their views and incorporate
their ideas, based on operational experience, into his designs. Because
of this a bond existed between the pilots and Fokker that produced
results denied to most other aircraft manufacturers. Fokker also
possessed an uncanny ability to perceive what changes were necessary
in a design to eradicate undesirable qualities and to promote improved
handling and performance. This was not merely an attribute of a
skilled pilot, but showed a sound knowledge of aerodynamics which
was put to good use in the experimental environment that obtained at
this time.

After the collapse of Germany in 1918 Fokker took several train-
loads of aircraft, engines and materials to Holland; these he claimed to
be his own property, since they had not been paid for by the German
government, and he was thus able to recommence his aircraft manufacturing business, now known as NV Nederlandsche Vliegtuigen-
fabriek, on 21 July 1919. He died in New York on 23 December 1939,
but his heritage lives on today in the Dutch aircraft manufacturing
company which bears his name. In recent years there have been
allegations that attempt to discredit the genius of this Dutch aircraft
constructor. I do not subscribe to these ideas, and, while admitting
that he may on occasion have been inspired by others, it is my belief
that the many fine fighting aeroplanes that emerged from the
Schwerin works during the First World War were products both of
endless experimentation and of the fertile mind of A. H. G. Fokker.

In this compilation an attempt has been made to indicate the
relative importance of each Fokker type, and a number of
experimental machines (not all successful) have also been included.
The photographs are from the author's collection, amassed over a
period of some forty years. This collection owes much to the industry
of other enthusiasts, and use has been made of photographs that
originated with Peter M. Bowers, Ed Ferko, Peter M. Grosz, Heinz J.
Nowarra, Bruno J. Schmäling, Bengt Wahlstrom, Egon Krüger, Bill
Puglisi and Willi Stiasny, the last three of whom are, sadly, no longer
with us.

Alex Imrie

3. Anthony Fokker in his third Spider (so called because the bracing-wire arrangement was likened to a spider's web). The accommodation is exposed, the necessary instruments being carried on the person. No ailerons were fitted to this aircraft, the handwheel on the control column operating the rudder. The engine is a 50hp water-cooled four-cylinder Argus with fully exposed gear train at the rear working the camshaft and single magneto. Note the gravity fuel tank in the front wing bracing pylon with its glass tube contents indicator.

4. A 100hp Argus-powered Spider in a steep bank over the Rumpler sheds at Johannisthal. Wing bracing is via one pylon, the previous rear wing bracing pylon having been moved aft of the pilot's seat to provide a kingpost for rear fuselage bracing. This model, with a fuselage fairing, was given the Fokker designation M1 ('M' meaning *Militär*, or military) and was delivered early in 1913.

▲3   ▼4

5. Fokker paid considerable attention to the successes of the Morane-Saulnier monoplane powered by the 50hp Gnome rotary engine, but although his M5, shown here, looked similar to the French aircraft it was engineered in an entirely different manner (one difference being that the Fokker fuselage was made from welded steel tube in place of the Morane's wooden structure). It was later designated M5K ('K' meaning *Kurz*, or short-span) since a version with increased wingspan became the M5L (*Lang*, or long-span).

6. Aerobatic demonstrations by Fokker on the M5L powered by the German-built 80hp Oberursel-Gnome rotary engine at Johannisthal caused a sensation, and by mid-1914 he was undoubtedly one of the most skilled pilots of the day. The military authorities quickly saw an application for this machine, and a number of Fokker M5Ls were ordered shortly before the outbreak of war.

7. After the outbreak of war in August 1914 a version of the M5L with a widened fuselage, to accommodate two crewmen in staggered side-by-side seats, was ordered. Of shoulder-wing configuration to improve downward observation, it was designated M8 by Fokker. Early in 1915 attempts were made to arm these machines: the installation shown here is a Mauser 25-shot semi-automatic rifle attached to a curved rail in the wing bracing pylon, with a fixed elevation to avoid the propeller.

5▲

6▲   7▼

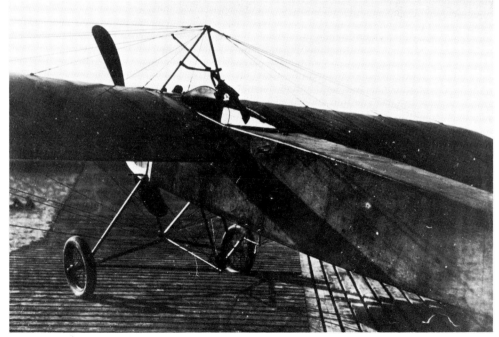

8. Following the capture on 19 April 1915 of Roland Garros, who had scored some successes against German aircraft by free-firing his machine gun through a Saulnier-armoured propeller, the German authorities learned with surprise that Fokker already had a gun-gear that worked! This is a demonstration model of Fokker's device, using a normal water-cooled infantry MG08. The high lobe on the cam, driven by the engine, operated the trigger when the 'missing link' was forced into place by pressure on the thumb push in the centre of the control column grip at lower centre left.

9. Fokker was given a Parabellum LMG14 (lightened machine-gun, 1914 model), fitted this to a Fokker M5K at Schwerin, and within forty-eight hours had adapted and adjusted the gun-gear to make it work satisfactorily. He was then able to demonstrate the device to officials of *Idflieg* (Inspectorate of Military Aviation) at Döberitz in air-to-ground firing. This is thought to be the original installation known as the M5K/MG, which was immediately ordered in quantity as the Fokker E ('E' meaning *Eindecker*, or monoplane armed with a machine gun).

10. Fokker was instructed to take the first aircraft of this type to the Front in order to introduce it to the operational flying units, qualified rotary-engine pilots being allowed to fly the aircraft. Fokker is seen here in May 1915 giving last-minute instructions to a two-seater pilot from *Feldfliegerabteilung 25* at Diedenhofen aerodrome. This machine is powered by the 100hp Oberursel UI and is Parabellum-armed; no Army serial number is visible, but this Fokker demonstrator was later numbered E3/15.

11. The Fokker *Gestängesteuerung* (pushrod control) was not a true interrupter gun-gear but more properly a synchronizer, the high lobe on the cam fitted to the engine allowing the gun to fire when the propeller blade was not in line with the weapon's muzzle. Owing to stiffness in the linkage and other causes, this primitive mechanism could allow the gun to fire at the wrong time, as is evident from this photograph, in which at least seven bullets have almost sawn off the wooden blade of a Fokker E monoplane's Garuda propeller.

▲12

12. The small size of the Fokker E monoplane (wingspan 8.9m) is emphasized in this rear view of *Unteroffizier* Kneiste's E 8/15 at Bucancy aerodrome during the summer of 1915. The forward cables provided the wing bracing, whilst the rear cables on the upper wing surface, routed via a small pulley in the wing bracing pylon, were merely for balance. The lower aft cables were connected to the control column via a rocking shaft and produced the actual warping of the wing surfaces for lateral control.

13. This Fokker E monoplane appears to have force-landed with a dead engine since the propeller has escaped damage; the pilot was lucky to wrap the left wing around a tree and so absorb the impact. The seven-cylinder Oberursel was a licence-made Gnome of only 80hp, and later many machines of this type were up-rated by having the more powerful Oberursel UI nine-cylinder engine of 100hp fitted.

▼13

14. *Leutnant* Max Immelmann of *Feldfliegerabteilung 62* at Douai in Fokker E 13/15. On 1 August 1915 he scored what is thought to have been the first official victory obtained on the Fokker monoplane, when he forced a BE2C to land. Because of a shortage of Parabellum LMG14s, Fokker caused the MG08 to be fitted with an air-cooled mantel (shown here) instead of the heavy water-cooled jacket, thus providing an ample supply of machine-guns (known as LMG08) that prevented delayed delivery of Fokker E monoplanes.

15. Although individual and unit markings were soon to become the norm on fighter aeroplanes, when the Fokker E monoplane was introduced they were not in general use: the fuselage marking and the name *Habicht* (Hawk), used by *Unteroffizier* Dietrich of *Feldfliegerabteilung 24* on E 6/15 is one of the earliest known examples. Note that this machine, in common with other early Fokker E monoplanes, is armed with the Parabellum LMG14.

▲16

16. An early attempt was made to improve the performance of the Fokker EI (roman numerals were used from August 1915 to distinguish between versions) by fitting the higher-powered Oberursel UI rotary engine of 100hp and by reducing the wingspan to increase the wing loading. This resulted in the Fokker EII, but it was not the success that had been hoped for and was only produced in small numbers, the maximum number at the Front being twenty, a figure reached in February 1916.

17. New wings of 9.52m span were fitted, and this resulted in the Fokker EIII, an example of which is seen here after taking off from an aerodrome on the Eastern Front. This became the most widely

manufactured version of the Fokker E monoplane, the highest number recorded at the Front being 110, at the end of April 1916. Experiments showed that it was not practical to fit two machine guns on the EIII – the loss in performance was too severe.

18. *Unteroffizier* Böhme of *Feldfliegerabteilung 9b* (left) assists with loading the LMG08 ammunition box of his Fokker EIII. The hemp belt held 550 rounds and the rate of fire was initially 400 rounds per minute. Böhme was one of the first German pilots to bring down two enemy aircraft in one day when on 25 September 1915, within the space of a few minutes, he brought down two out of a formation of three French Farman bombing machines attacking Freiburg.

▼17

18▶

▲ 19

19. *Leutnant* Bruno Loerzer, of *Feldfliegerabteilung 25*, taking off in Fokker EII 20/15. Note the amount of smoke produced by the half-burnt castor lubricating oil. All rotary-engined aircraft threw out a great deal of oil, earning them the nickname *'Sardinenkisten'* (sardine boxes) amongst pilots and mechanics alike.

20. This unarmed Fokker EI, marked with the Army designation

03.51, was one of a batch of twenty-eight Fokker aircraft of different types supplied to the Austro-Hungarian Army at the end of 1915. It was transferred from the German Air Service, where its identity was Fokker EI 64/15. The outlined rudder cross is unusual at this time.

▼ 20

21. Naval landplane units also operated Fokker E monoplanes. The first naval pilot to undergo the conversion course at *Kampfeinsitzer-abteilung I* at Mannheim was *Flugmaat* Boedicker, seen here in December 1915 in the first naval Fokker EI. The aircraft was attached to *II Marine Landfliegerabteilung* at Nieumunster in Flanders.

22. The first Fokker EIV was earmarked for Immelmann, who wanted a triple-gun installation. The wing area was increased still further when wings of 10m span were fitted, and the forward fuselage was strengthened to take the 160hp Oberursel UIII 14-cylinder double-row rotary engine. There were continual problems with the gun-gear, and although the type was reportedly flown with success by Immelmann subsequent Fokker EIVs were fitted with only two guns. Overheating of the large engine also occurred, and additional ventilation slots were cut in the front cowlings of production machines.

▲23

23. A close-up photograph of the forward fuselage of the three-gun Fokker EIV, showing the tubular steel structure necessary for the front bearing of its heavy rotary engine. The push-rods for the machine-gun synchronizing gear from the cam on the rear of the engine can be seen, as can the disposition of the aluminium ammunition boxes. Note how the guns are inclined upwards at 15 degrees, a practice continued on the twin-gun version that drew adverse comment from some pilots.

24. Initially, Fokker E monoplanes were attached singly to the two-seater units, but from late 1915 it was found that better results were obtained by operating the single-seaters in groups. This concentration led to the non-permanent formations known as *Kampfeinsitzer-kommandos* (single-seater fighter detachments) which were formed

or dissolved as the tactical situation demanded. It was not merely the use in numbers that mattered: of more consequence was strict in-flight discipline, in order that pilots assist rather than impede each other during a fight.

25. In order to prevent gun mechanisms freezing at low temperatures, canvas covers were sometimes used, as seen here on *Leutnant* Walter von Bülow's Fokker EII 25/15 of *Feldfliegerabteilung 22*.

26. Victor and vanquished: *Vizefeldwebel* Wäss, of *Feldflieger-abteilung 3*, proudly stands in the nacelle of the FE2b that he forced to land on 22 February 1916 whilst flying the Fokker EIII on the left. Note the double-barrelled signal pistol attached to the right-hand side of the cockpit.

▼24

▲27 ▼28

27. The only German aeroplanes that were started by hand-swinging the propeller were those that were powered by rotary engines. This mechanic is obviously starting the Oberursel UI of Fokker EIII 401/15 of *Fokkerstaffel Jametz* for test purposes, since the cowling has been removed. Note how all the aluminium panels, including the front bulkhead, are 'engine-turned' to prevent corrosion. The small windmill-driven pump for pressurizing the fuel system can be seen on the front left strut of the undercarriage trestle.

28. One of Fokker's armament mechanics, who periodically visited units in the field to supervise and adjust the LMG08 and its gun-gear, working on the gun of Fokker EIII 615/15. This personal attention was responsible for increasing the gun's rate of fire from 400 to 600 rounds per minute. The machine has been raised into a flying position so that the barrel of the LMG08 can be aligned with the aircraft's fore-and-aft axis.

29. *Oberleutnant* Buddecke, wearing a tropical helmet, with Fokker

EIII 96/15, which appears to have been overpainted. The aircraft is marked with Turkish national insignia, formed by the simple expedient of completely painting out the original German iron crosses. The photograph was probably taken at the aerodrome at Chanak-Kale after a German single-seater element sent to Gallipoli had been absorbed into the Turkish *Fliegerabteilung 6*.

30. The remains of *Oberleutnant* Max Immelmann's Fokker EIII in the hangar at Douai. When he was killed on 18 June 1916 he had been officially credited with fifteen victories and was known as 'The Eagle of Lille'. The German crash investigation team found that the failure of Immelmann's gun-gear had caused the loss of one propeller blade which had resulted in manoeuvres that overstressed the airframe. Note the straight break on the left-hand propeller blade, exactly in line with the machine-gun muzzle, and the flattened steel tube longerons on the rear fuselage, showing evidence of bending that gives credence to the German findings.

▲31 ▼32

31. There was no instrument panel as such on the Fokker E monoplanes. This view of the cockpit of a captured EIII shows the Bosch ignition switch at top left, the Morell Phalax rpm indicator immediately below, and the fine adjustment for the carburettor below that. The hand-pump on the right cockpit wall was for pressurizing the fuel tank situated behind the pilot, in order to transfer fuel to a small gravity tank forward from which the engine was fed. Although not visible in this photograph, an oil pulsator glass on the right, plus a fuel contents gauge on the coaming in front of the windscreen and a magnetic compass in the right wing root, completed the instrument array.

32. In order to safeguard the mechanics of the synchronized machine gun, Fokker E monoplane pilots had strict orders not to cross the front lines, a policy wrongly interpreted by the Allies, who thought that the German pilots had 'cold feet'! Eventually, on 6 April 1916, a Fokker E pilot lost his bearings and landed on the British side of the lines, and the secret was out: this is his machine, Fokker EIII 210/16, at St-Omer in British markings. Just how flexible were the warping wings is evidenced by the air mechanic on the right pulling on the aft wing warping cable. This aircraft exists today in the Science Museum in London.

33. *Hauptmann* Oswald Boelcke with his Fokker EIV. The additional cooling holes in the front cowling and the streamlined rear-view mirror fitted under the wing bracing pylon are visible in this photograph. Boelcke first flew Fokker E monoplanes with Immelmann at Douai, but later spent much of his time in the Verdun area. He had scored nineteen victories in aerial combat by the end of June 1916, when, following the death of Immelmann, he was officially rested for a period and removed from flying operations.

34. The necessity of replacing the Fokker E monoplanes caused Fokker to embark on a systematic evaluation of the compact biplane configuration. He did this by producing single and two-bay versions of designs that were powered by rotary and stationary engines and fitting these with wing warping or ailerons. The first machine was designated M16E ('E' meaning *Einstielig*, or single-bay). It was powered by the 100hp Mercedes water-cooled six-cylinder engine and employed wing warping for lateral control.

33▲   34▼

▲35

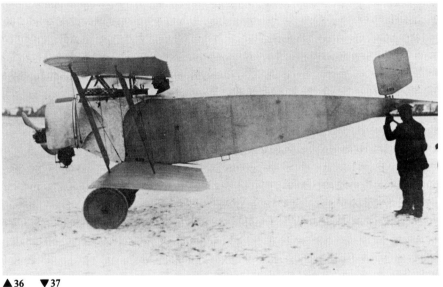

▲36　▼37

35. The Fokker M17E, seen here in its original form with narrow-gap, unstaggered wings with wing warping, was a rotary-powered version of the M16E and used the 100hp Oberursel UI. It was armed with one LMG08 and had a steel tube crash pylon over the cockpit to protect the pilot in the event of the aircraft turning over on landing.

36. A much-modified M17E was built with the wing gap increased by fitting a normal centre-section and the wings themselves staggered to improve the view from the cockpit. Lateral control was still by wing warping, and the armament consisted of one LMG08.

37. The Fokker M18ZK ('Z' meaning *Zweistielig*, or two-bay, and 'K' standing for *Klappenverwindung*, or aileron control) was initially powered by the Mercedes 100hp water-cooled engine, with 'ear' radiators fitted on the fuselage sides adjacent to the lower wing leading edge. The ailerons were horn-balanced and the rear end of the fuselage terminated in a point. After modifications that included a reversion to the Fokker E monoplane fuselage stern and tail unit, the type was ordered as the Fokker DI, when it was re-engined with the 120hp Mercedes and armed with one LMG08.

38. Denied higher-powered engines, Fokker was compelled to build very light airframes in order to extract the maximum performance from the 120hp Mercedes, and his fighter biplanes drew heavily on the E monoplane's construction techniques. The Fokker DI, ordered in May 1916, reached the Front in July, and by the end of October there were 74 serving with the newly established fighter formations. Like most of the machines of this type that saw operational service, aircraft 151/16, from *Jagdstaffel 1*, was fitted with a large triangular fin to improve its directional stability.

39. The circular plywood disc bolted to the propeller hub was used as a guide when calibrating the synchronizing gun-gear and also showed the angular movement between the engine actuating the trigger and the passage of the bullet between the blades. In this photograph, Fokker is standing on the wheel of an early DI, whilst at the far right *Hauptmann* Boelcke and *Leutnant* Frankl, whose final victory scores were 40 and 18 respectively, are seen in conversation.

▲40　▼41

40. The Fokker DII was the production version of the M17ZF ('F' meaning *Flächenverwindung*, or wing warping). It was powered by the 100hp Oberursel UI rotary engine in place of the Fokker DI's six-cylinder water-cooled engine of 120hp, and there was little to choose between the performance of the two machines. Sixteen Fokker DIIs were at the Front by the end of August, and this figure had increased to 68 by the end of the year. Note the raised centre section to improve the pilot's field of view forward, and the single LMG08/15 offset to starboard.

41. Fokker DII 559/16, packed for transit to the Front. At this time aircraft were painted with camouflage colours on their top surfaces only, the sides and under-surfaces remaining in clear doped finish. Note the propeller in its canvas cover under the fuselage and the interplane struts bundled into the centre-section. The machine is one of the wing-warping type and the very thin aerofoil sections common with this feature can be seen.

42. *Leutnant* Kissenberth, of *Feldfliegerabteilung 9b*, flying his Fokker DII, 540/16, over Colmar. This machine has had additional camouflage applied in the field, including the removal of the large white backgrounds to the national insignia on the upper wing. Note how uneven the white borders to the black crosses have become; according to regulations, they should have been 5cm (approx 2in) wide.

43. In order to improve perfor-mance and to allow the carriage of the desired two-gun armament, the Fokker DIII was produced. It was basically a Fokker DII modified to use the 160hp Oberursel UIII 14-cylinder, two-row rotary engine. However, during the early months of 1917 Fokker fighter biplanes were phased out of front-line operations because of structural faults – the price paid by Fokker for using flimsy construction techniques in his constant battle to improve power-to-weight ratios. Fokker DIII 1601/16, seen here, has turned over on to its back as a result of the broken undercarriage, possibly brought about by a heavy landing.

44. Fokker DIII 379/16 was one of a batch of ten supplied by Germany to Holland in October 1917; it became No. 201 in service with the *Luchtvaartafdeling* (LVA, or Dutch Army Air Service). Note that the orange discs of the Dutch national markings have been applied over the standard white backgrounds of the German 'iron cross' type markings.

42 ▲

43 ▲   44 ▼

▲45

45. Fokker's M20 became the DIV in production. It was powered by the 160hp Mercedes and was basically a Fokker DI improved to take the more powerful engine. Twin guns were fitted, and lateral control was by means of horn-balanced ailerons fitted to the top wing only. Two machines of the type were at the Front at the end of August, and in early September an additional forty were ordered, the majority of which were, however, used only in non-operational roles.

46. Sold to Sweden in March 1918, this Fokker DIV, 5851/17, was one of four aircraft fitted with the 150hp Benz engine. Although having an improved all-round performance over the earlier Fokker D biplanes, the Fokker DIV was produced at a time when the frequency of accidents to Fokker-built aircraft had increased to unacceptable proportions, causing their removal from the Front. As a result, this design was possibly not as carefully evaluated as it might otherwise have been.

▼46

47. Although Fokker's M22 was also made with two-bay wings and wing-warping for lateral control, it was the M22EK that went into production as the Fokker DV. A great deal of attention had been given to streamlining the fuselage, which was multi-stringered aft of a completely circular cowling around the 100hp Oberursel UI. The large spinner around the propeller boss was essential for efficient engine cooling.

48. Despite its minimal engine power and corresponding low performance, the Fokker DV handled well and was reputedly the best Fokker single-seater built up to the end of 1916. It went into production in November and a few machines served with front-line units. The German Naval Air Service also had a number for *Hallenschutz* (airship shed protection) duties, such as this example employed at the Naval Air Station at Hage. Note the numeral '1' under the starboard wing tip.

▲49

49. Three Fokker DVs and one DIII lined up at the aerodrome at Schleissheim during the summer of 1917; the aircraft are part of the equipment of *Sturmstaffel I* under *Oberleutnant* Justinius and intended for the aerial defence of Munich. The group of visiting dignitaries includes *Generalleutnant* von Hoeppner and *Oberst-leutnant* Thomsen, who were, respectively, the Commanding General of the Air Service and his Chief of Staff.

50. This armed Fokker DV, with fuselage decoration and strut streamers, is almost certainly from one of the *Kampfeinsitzerstaffeln* (single-seater fighter units) employed in the aerial defence of Germany's western borders.

51. Fokker was obviously inspired by Junkers' all-metal cantilever wings and undertook to make similar wooden structures. This was

his first plywood-covered cantilever wing to fly, fitted to an unbraced sesquiplane which has remarkably modern lines for early 1917. The control surfaces were aerodynamically balanced extremities of the surfaces themselves. This machine, built at the time as a private venture, failed to arouse official interest, although Fokker stated that it was 'fast and sensitive'.

52. A new wing with a swept-back leading edge and having even more depth than that previously built was fitted to a sesquiplane powered by a six-cylinder water-cooled engine. The poor forward view evident here was later improved by raising the upper wing, and a conventional fin and rudder were fitted. The experience gained paved the way for other cantilever wing structures, including those used on Fokker's large commercial monoplanes of the 1920s.

▼50

▲53　▼54

53. The first Fokker triplane was of very short span, did not have any interplane struts and featured unbalanced ailerons and elevators; powered by the 110hp Le Rhône rotary engine, it must have been tricky to fly. It was built in the space of a few weeks, before official triplane orders were placed by *Idflieg* with any manufacturer. Note the hefty box spars, visible through the translucent fabric, that allowed the wings to be of true cantilever construction.

54. *Leutnant* Werner Voss seated in the first Fokker triplane at Schwerin. It was probably information from Voss that caused Manfred von Richthofen to state on 18 July 1917, from his hospital bed (where he was recovering from a wound in the head), that Fokker had a triplane design all ready and that it had good speed and climb characteristics which 'should be encouraged'.

55▲ 56▼

55. The next Fokker triplane was of increased wing area and had balanced control surfaces. Its wing cellule had thin spruce interplane struts of little structural strength that were possibly only fitted to reduce the amplitude of wing vibration. On test, and with a full military load, the aircraft reached an altitude of 16,400ft in 18 minutes. A fighter's rate of climb was at this time considered to be more important than mere speed, and an official order was placed for three experimental machines of the type early in July 1917.

56. A close-up photograph of the cockpit and twin LMG08/15 armament on the modified Fokker triplane prototype. Note the complete absence of 'clutter': the only wires to be seen are the diagonal bracing across the front centre-section struts and the aileron operating cables running up to the top wing. The triplane's excellent manoeuvrability, which made it a superb dog-fighter, stemmed not so much from the triplane configuration as from its lightweight, aerodynamically clean structure and the characteristics of the rotary engine.

57. The first two Fokker triplanes to go to the Front were of the V4 type ('V' meaning *Versuchsflugzeug*, or experimental aircraft); they received the military designations FI 102/17 and FI 103/17. They differed only slightly from later production versions and, for example, did not have the wing-tip skids which were a feature of all subsequent Fokker triplanes. One of the V4 machines is seen here being flown at Schwerin, probably by Fokker himself.

58. Fokker seated in one of his pre-production triplanes at Marckebeeke aerodrome near Courtrai in Flanders – the base of *Jagdgeschwader I*. He is speaking to *General* von Lossberg, the Chief of Staff of the German IV Army. *Rittmeister* Manfred von Richthofen and *Leutnant* Adam look on, whilst in the background can be seen a Fokker DV assigned to the unit for training transition from the Albatros DV to the rotary-engined Fokker triplane.

59. *Leutnant* Werner Voss with Fokker FI 103/17. This aircraft was powered by a captured Le Rhône engine previously fitted to a Nieuport Scout, and the shape of the cowling lent itself to decoration such as has been tastefully carried out here. Voss, *Staffelführer* of *Jagdstaffel 10*, had a final victory score close to fifty; he obtained ten of those in September 1917, a number of them on the triplane, before he was killed in this machine on the 23rd of the month in a single-handed fight against seven pilots from No. 56 Squadron RFC.

57▶

▼58

59▶

▲60   ▼61

34

60. Fokker's policy of developing both rotary- and stationary-engined experimental examples of the same aircraft resulted in the fitting of a six-cylinder Mercedes engine to a modified triplane known as the V6. When this was unsuccessful, further attempts were made by moving the triplane wing cellule well forward, lengthening the fuselage and fitting a biplane tandem wing arrangement immediately behind the cockpit. This resulted in the V8, shown here. Reputedly flown twice by Fokker in late 1917, the type was not proceeded with.

61. Although the Fokker DrI triplane was immensely strong it also had problems, due initially to weak aileron attachments aggravated by poor gluing procedures which were further degraded by the ingress of moisture. *Leutnant* Heinrich Gontermann of *Jagdstaffel 15*, who had 39 confirmed aerial victories, was killed at La Neuville aerodrome on 29 October 1917 flying 115/17: the loss of the right-hand aileron was followed by the shedding of ribs and fabric, and the aircraft went out of control. The double-box spar of the failed upper wing remained intact until ground impact.

62. In order that the aircraft industry could concentrate on the best fighter designs, manufacturers were encouraged to compete in comparative flight tests at Adlershof, near Berlin. The first of these was held in January 1918 and eight Fokker designs were entered in the various sections. The V9 cantilever sesquiplane, powered by the 110hp Le Rhône and relying heavily on Fokker DrI triplane practice, was demonstrated but not flown in competition.

63. Also at the first fighter competition were two versions of the V13; related to the V9, these were powered by the Oberursel UrIII and the Siemens-Halske ShIII shown here. Although these 160hp engines were not yet ready for front-line service an order was placed in March for 120 production aircraft of this type, to be powered by the Oberursel UrII of 110hp. That this aircraft, known as the Fokker DVI, was seen as a mere stop-gap is shown by the cancellation of sixty of those machines in favour of the Fokker EV parasol in May 1918.

64. The forward fuselage of the Fokker V7 triplane. Powered by the 160hp Siemens-Halske ShIII counter-rotary engine, this aircraft was also present at the first fighter competition although it was not flown in the trials. Note the forward support bearing for the engine, the position of the fuel tank and the dispersed nature of the cockpit fittings. It was necessary to lengthen the undercarriage on this machine to provide ground clearance for the enormous propeller.

62 ▲

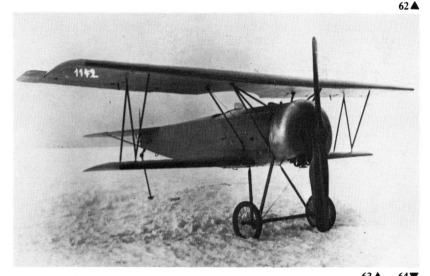

63 ▲   64 ▼

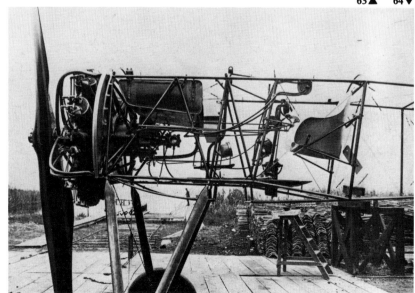

▲ 65

65. Even a light aeroplane like the Fokker DrI triplane, which weighed only 829lb (376kg) empty, could be difficult to push around on muddy aerodromes. Here 'man's best friend' is being utilized to move a machine belonging to *Jagdstaffel 12*, a component of *Jagdgeschwader II* at Toulis aerodrome, March 1918.

66. *Hauptmann* Adolf Ritter von Tutscheck, who was officially credited with 27 aerial victories, was the *Kommandeur* of *Jagdgeschwader II* and is seen here in his Fokker DrI triplane, 404/17, the machine in which he was killed on 15 March 1918. It is marked with the colours of his old unit, *Jagdstaffel 12* – white nose cowling and black tail unit – although later the white cross backgrounds on rudder and fuselage were painted black, leaving only the regulation 5cm wide white border. Note the anemometer-type airspeed indicator on the port wing interplane strut and the wing-tip streamers attached to the lower wing trailing edge.

67. A three-quarter rear view of Fokker DrI triplane 512/17,

showing the camouflage finish in which these aircraft left the factory – streaky, dirty greenish-brown uppersurfaces and light blue undersurfaces. The national insignia are displayed on white backgrounds, a style that regulations define as being out of date from October 1916. Note how the undersurface colour is extended around the tailplane and elevator outline and on the bottom fuselage longerons.

68. *Leutnant* Richard Kraut sitting in an unarmed Fokker DrI triplane, 422/17, at *Jagdstaffelschule I* (Fighter School No. 1) at Valenciennes in July 1918. Aircraft used for fighting instruction were normally veterans of service with the front-line units, and as such were well decorated with the colourful markings of their previous owners. This machine shows no evidence of having been used in this way, although the out-of-date rudder and fuselage crosses show signs of having been changed.

▼ 66

69. The cockpit and twin LMG08/15 armament of a Fokker DrI triplane of *Jagdstaffel 12*, showing the use of a reflector sight made by the Oigee company of Berlin. Note the rear-view mirror, the cut-down windscreen between the guns and the signal cartridge rack on the right-hand side of the fuselage. The tube adjacent to the rack and projecting from the fuselage is the muzzle of the signal pistol, whilst between the gun butts an altimeter has been suspended. The chutes feeding the guns carry the cartridges in a hemp belt, which is collected in a box fed via the chutes on the left-hand side of the guns; spent cartridges were discharged overboard.

70. NCO pilot *Vizefeldwebel* (Acting Sergeant Major) Otto Esswein poses with the complete establishment of Fokker DrI triplanes belonging to *Jagdstaffel 26*. The form of national insignia shows that the photograph was taken after the official change from iron cross to straight-sided cross, which came into effect on 17 March 1918. Signal cartridges can be seen in the cockpit racks, with the projecting muzzle of the signal pistol immediately below.

71. Fokker DrI triplane 581/17 in French hands and painted in French camouflage colours. The number displayed on the tricolour-painted rudder, 2251, is the original Fokker works number for this machine. Note that the machine guns have been removed and that a Nieuport engine, cowling and propeller have been substituted for the original German items. The scalloped trailing edges of the flying surfaces – caused by the trailing-edge wire being pulled in between the tails of the ribs by the tautness of the doped fabric – are seen to advantage in this view.

72. The Richthofen brothers pose by a Fokker DrI triplane. Manfred, on the left, was the leading German fighter pilot, with eighty confirmed victories to his credit when he was killed in aerial combat flying Fokker DrI triplane 425/17; his brother Lothar, who had forty confirmed victories, survived the war. Both are considered to have been Fokker DrI triplane aces, yet each only achieved a relatively small number of his victories on this machine.

73. Although superseded by machines of higher performance, the Fokker DrI triplane did not completely disappear from front-line units, and some were still in use operationally at the end of the war. From the 320 machines produced, the greatest number recorded at the Front, 171, was realized at the end of April 1918; the bulk of these aircraft were in service with the three large fighting formations, *Jagdgeschwadern I*, *II* and *III*. The photograph shows *Leutnant* Janzen of *Jagdstaffel 6*, in Richthofen's *Jagdgeschwader I*, with his machine, Fokker DrI 403/17.

74. With the coming of the Fokker DVII in April 1918, the Fokker DrI triplanes of the élite *Jagdgeschwadern* found their way to lesser formations; shown is *Leutnant* Rudolf Stark, of *Jagdstaffel 34b*, with a DrI previously used by *Jagdgeschwader I*, 14 May 1918. Note that its 'iron cross'-type national insignia have been changed to *Balkenkreuz*-type straight-sided crosses, as laid down in the official instructions dated 17 March 1918 (compliance with which was required before 15 April 1918).

75. Fokker V11, said to have been the 160hp six-cylinder water-cooled Mercedes-powered version of the Fokker V9, had a two-spar bottom wing and used steel tube 'N' interplane struts. Winner of its class in the first fighter comparative flying meeting at Adlershof, it was developed and produced in numbers as the Fokker DVII. During the competition it climbed to 5,000m (16,400ft) in 25.2 minutes.

▲72　▼73

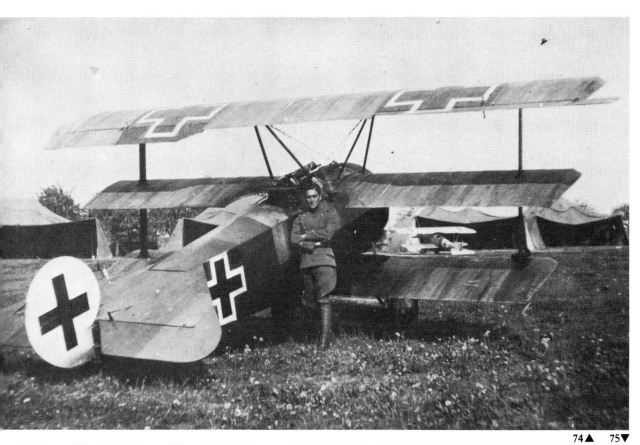

74▲   75▼

▲76

76. Another step in the Fokker DVII development story produced the Fokker V18, which was also flown at the first fighter competition in the 160hp Mercedes class. Although its time for the 5,000m climb was 28 minutes, this machine is said to have scored additional points for manoeuvrability. The fin appears to have been retrospectively fitted, obviously to aid the machine's directional stability. The Morell anemometer-type airspeed indicator can be seen at the port interplane strut, while a 'test pilot's panel' is fitted just ahead of the cockpit.

77. Initial production Fokker DVIIs were finished in exactly the same manner as the Fokker DrI triplane – streaked over all upper and side surfaces with dirty greenish/brown dope and showing out-of-date national insignia in the form of iron crosses on large white backgrounds at the usual locations. It has been recorded that the experimental airframes V11 and V18 were completed to the standard shown here after the Adlershof meeting.

78. *Jagdstaffel 10 (Jagdgeschwader I)* received some of the first production Fokker DVIIs. This machine, 234/18, flown by

Leutnant Friedrichs, overran the landing area and collided with two parked Fokker DVIIs and some tents before coming to rest on its nose, revealing its mainplane to be covered with four-colour 'lozenge' printed camouflage fabric. The national insignia displayed on the wing has finally received the 5cm wide white border, the regulations for which had been in force since October 1916. However, a new directive in force from 17 March 1918 called for all crosses to have straight sides, and on this aircraft the easily accessible crosses on fuselage and rudder have already been changed from the factory-applied 'iron cross' type.

79. This Fokker DVI, 1631/18, on acceptance flying at Adlershof in April 1918, is marked with the regulation 15cm white surround to the straight-sided crosses as defined in the 17 March 1918 directive. This gave the fuselage crosses a peculiarly exaggerated effect that would be changed again by the issue of two more directives on the subject. The complete airframe is covered in four-colour 'lozenge' printed camouflage fabric, light shades on the undersurface and dark shades on the uppersurfaces.

▼77

▲ 80

80. To guard against possible shortages of steel tubing, three experimental Fokker DVIIs with wooden fuselages were built, two by Fokker and one (the example shown here) by Albatros-Gesellschaft für Flugzeugunternehmungen mbH at Johannisthal near Berlin. In the event, steel tube remained available and there was no need to resort to wood for the fuselages of production aircraft.

81. In order to ensure that as many Fokker DVIIs were produced in

as short a time as possible, it was necessary to seek sub-contractors to augment the Fokker production line. The Albatros company at Johannisthal near Berlin and its sister-company Ostdeutsche Albatroswerke GmbH (OAW) at Schneidemühl in Pomerania were awarded large contracts that eventually resulted in their producing more aircraft than the parent factory. Three machines from the first production batch from OAW are seen here with engine cowlings removed and awaiting final acceptance inspection.

▼ 81

82▲

82. The angular aggressiveness of the Fokker DVII, the finest fighter of the war, is apparent in this flying view. Powered by the BMW IIIa six-cylinder engine, the DVII could climb to 6,000m (19,600ft) in 21 minutes, was capable of 122mph and remained highly manoeuvrable even at its ceiling. Many Allied pilots took the opportunity to fly captured aircraft after the end of the war, and almost without exception they agreed that a well-flown DVII was able to hold its own against any other fighter.

83. *Vizefeldwebel* Willi Gabriel, of *Jagdstaffel 11*, with his Fokker DVII 256/18. Gabriel, who survived the war, scored a total of eleven victories, four of them on 18 July 1918. His aircraft had the typical streaked finish on the fuselage, whilst the mainplanes were covered in four-colour 'lozenge' printed fabric. Unit markings comprised red nose cowlings, struts and wheels, and Gabriel's personal markings consisted of light blue and orange stripes on top and bottom surfaces of tailplane and elevators.

83▼

▲84 ▼85

84. *Leutnant* Oliver *Freiherr* von Beaulieu-Marconnay, of *Jagdstaffel 15*, his Fokker DVII emblazoned with the sign that was used in his old regiment (4th Dragoons) as a branding iron symbol for its horses. The unit markings consisted of a blue overpainted fuselage and tail unit, with the forward part of the fuselage, including the engine cowlings, painted red. It is not easy to see where the colour division is in this view, but a vertical line can just be discerned at the mid-cockpit position. Note the rear-view mirror, the windscreen with aiming holes and the large rpm indicator in the cockpit just beneath the machine-gun butts.

85. *Leutnant* Josef Raesch (*Jagdstaffel 43*) in his Fokker DVII and accompanied by his mechanics. The unit markings consisted of white tail units, fuselages of various colours, and fuselage symbols for individual identification. As can be seen, the white on this machine terminates at an oblique line at the cockpit, which location is marked with a three-pronged fork head. Raesch survived the war and was credited with six victories. He was shot down in flames on

this aircraft on 25 July 1918, but his life was saved by one of the recently introduced Heinecke parachutes.

86. *Leutnant* Lothar *Freiherr* von Richthofen with his father, *Major* Albrecht *Freiherr* von Richthofen, with Fokker DVII 244/18, July 1918. Note that the proportions of the national insignia indicate that this machine left the factory with 'iron crosses', these being altered in the field to comply with the changes already mentioned; the wing crosses also reveal the original iron-cross outline. Tailplane and elevators are chequered in black and white, whilst the nose cowling would have been painted yellow. This machine was previously flown by *Leutnant* Heldmann, of *Jagdstaffel 10*.

87. Five Fokker DVIIs from *Jagdstaffel 11*, about to leave Bengneux aerodrome, July 1918. *Vizefeldwebel* Gabriel's machine now sports a fuselage stripe in orange and has the rear of its fuselage striped with orange and light blue. He is seen at the port wing tip, donning flying kit, and beside the next machine can be seen *Oberleutnant* von Wedel, who later became the leader of this unit.

▲88

▼89

88. Fokker DVIIs from the Schwerin production line were fitted with the BMW IIIa engine of 185hp as delivery of this fine power unit allowed. These aircraft can be identified by the 'F' in their military designation, as seen here on Fokker DVII F 461/18 at the Adlershof test centre near Berlin. Note the different styles of national insignia, that on the top surface of the mainplane adhering to the final instruction issued on this subject which was current on 4 June 1918.

89. A close-up view of the LMG08/15 installation on a Fokker DVII, showing the fuel and oil filler caps with oil-soaked fabric immediately below. The additional air scoop just below the aileron operating cable outlet is an attempt to alleviate the heating problem that caused self-ignition of the phosphorous ammunition during warm weather: in July 1918 several machines were lost when exploding cartridges ignited the nearby fuel tanks. There was a prohibition on the carriage of this ammunition from 22 July until the difficulty had been resolved.

90. A captured Fokker DVII on test, showing a British pitot head on the port interplane strut with its corresponding tubing running along the upper wing leading edge to the cockpit instrument. This machine was built by OAW and shows the later type of offset vertical filler pipe for the radiator. The object on top of the radiator is the camshaft-driven pump which supplied air to pressurize the fuel system. Later models of this pump were of the horizontal flat-twin type and were not as prominent as this vertical single-cylinder version.

91. There were a number of structural problems with Fokker DVIIs, especially where violent combat manoeuvres caused centre-section ribs aft of the main spar to fail in shear. Since this was in the slipstream area, the failures resulted in the almost complete destruction of the upper mainplane centre section, but the spars held and there are no records of fatalities attributable to this defect. The problem was soon rectified.

▲ 92   ▼ 93

94 ▲

◀95

92. The majority of Fokker DVIs were assigned to either training duties or home defence. The aircraft were powered by the Oberursel UrII rotary engine of 110hp, but their performance was no longer good enough for the front line. Steps were taken to re-fit the DVI with a higher-powered rotary engine, but in the event few machines seem to have been so modified and production was terminated in favour of the highly successful Fokker DVII and the Fokker EV parasol. Only 27 Fokker DVIs are recorded as being at the Front at the end of August 1918.

93. A further development of the V9 design that tried to improve on the Fokker DVI's shortcomings was the V33. Smaller and lighter than the DVI, the machine also appears structurally simpler, lacking balanced ailerons and elevators. It was not, however, proceeded with, although Fokker himself liked the machine and is reported to have taken it with him to Holland after the war.

94. Although the fuselage of this Fokker DVII is overpainted, the disposition of the national insignia indicates that the aircraft is a late Albatros-built machine. The coloured bands behind the cockpit are probably in the German colours of black, white and red. Note the wing-tip streamer and the fact that both sides of the fabric covers over the spoked wheels are decorated with national insignia-style crosses.

95. A close-up photograph of the uncowled nose of Fokker DVII (Alb) 5324/18, showing the installation of the 165hp Mercedes DIII six-cylinder engine. Note the two water pipes, one from each side of the radiator, joining and running aft to the engine-driven water pump. The radiator filler is centrally located, and the camshaft-driven air pump on this machine is of the Duplex flat-twin type. One of the features of the Fokker DVII radiator was that it could be changed, or removed for working on the engine, without the necessity of having to remove the propeller.

▲ 96

▲ 97   ▼ 98

96. A further development of the Fokker DVII was the V36, powered by the 185hp BMW IIIa engine enclosed in a completely redesigned nose with an oval radiator. A special feature was the location of the main fuel tank in the streamlined undercarriage spreader bar fairing, an attempt to move the dangers of burning petrol away from the main aeroplane structure. The machine was entered in the third fighter competition held at Adlershof in October 1918, and proved to be faster and had a better rate of climb than the BMW-powered Fokker DVII, going to 5,000m in 13½ minutes. At this late stage of the war it was not ordered into production.

97. The Armistice Treaty demanded the surrender of 2,000 German fighter and bomber aeroplanes. The Fokker DVII was singled out by name, but many aircraft of this type were flown back to Germany in defiance of the order. Seen here are five Fokker DVIIs of *Jagdstaffel 58* being burned at Champles aero-drome in November 1918 to prevent them falling into Allied hands. Despite this, the unit did deliver eight similar aircraft to Nivelles aerodrome in a gesture of compliance.

98. Major A. E. McKeever DSO MC, the greatest Allied two-seater pilot of the war, was officially credited with thirty victories and is seen here with Fokker DVII (OAW) 8493/18 at Shoreham just after hostilities ended. The machine is marked with insignia consisting of the figure '1' on a maple leaf – the marking used by No. 1 Squadron, Canadian Air Force, on its Sopwith Dolphin fighters. The table of weights adjacent to the cockpit shows that the aircraft weighed 700kg (1,540lb) empty and 880kg (1,936lb) loaded. These figures were not actual weights, but averages from a production batch.

99. An Albatros-built Fokker DVII in use by the 9th United States Aero Squadron during the winter of 1918. The machine has been completely over-painted, possibly in aluminium dope, but retains the German national insignia on the upper mainplane. The insignia of the 9th Aero Squadron is executed in red, white and blue, which colours are also used on the diagonal fuselage stripe running aft from the cockpit.

100. A daring concept for a fighter aeroplane in 1918 – the aerodynamically clean Fokker V28, seen here at the second fighter competition at Adlershof in June 1918 and fitted with the Oberursel UrII 110hp rotary engine. Although the V28 was adjudged the best entry, production versions of the aircraft (known as the Fokker EV) were beset with catastrophic structural failures of the plywood-covered cantilever wing and the type was grounded after only a few days' operational service in August. By the end of that month a total of eighty aircraft of this type had reached front-line units.

101. The fine lines of the Fokker V28 were not spoiled by the slightly bulged cowling fitted over the 11-cylinder Oberursel UrIII 160hp engine. In competition flying this airframe was successively fitted with three different engines, and with the Goebel GoeIII 160hp rotary, at a take-off weight of 1,336lb, climbed to 5,000m in just under 10½ minutes.

99 ▲

100 ▲   101 ▼

▲102

102. Anthony Fokker was on hand in August 1918 when the first consignment of Fokker EV parasol fighters arrived at *Armeeflugpark 7* for distribution amongst *Jagdgeschwadern I, II* and *III* in the area. *Jagdgeschwader II*, based at Chéry-les-Pouilly, received a number earmarked for *Jagdstaffel 19*, and this photograph shows Fokker doing his usual publicity stunt with 24 pilots and mechanics from *Jastas 12* and *19* on the cantilever wing to demonstrate the strength of the structure.

103. *Oberleutnant* Loewenhardt, of *Jagdstaffel 10*, took the chance to try out this new Fokker EV parasol fighter belonging to *Jagdstaffel 6* at Puisieux-Ferme, Chambry, early in August 1918. Every pilot who flew the parasol was full of praise for its great manoeuvrability, short take-off run, excellent rate of climb and good cockpit view.

104. Nine sleek Fokker EV parasols resplendent in the black and white unit markings of *Jagdstaffel 6* in *Jagdgeschwader Freiherr von Richthofen Nr I*, lined up with the remaining four Fokker DVIIs on Bernes aerodrome in the German 2nd Army area in front of Amiens, mid-August 1918. The nearest machine is EV 153/18, flown by the *Staffelführer, Leutnant* Richard Wenzl, who has marked his aircraft with fuselage bands in the proportions of the Iron Cross ribbon but with the colours reversed for personal identification.

▲106

105. (Previous spread) Fokker DVIIs of *Jagdgeschwader II* on the
aerodrome at Chéry-les-Pouilly, late 1918. The five nearest aircraft
are from *Jagdstaffel 15*, that with the winged arrow being flown by
the *Staffelführer, Leutnant* Josef Veltjens. The machines lined up in
the middle distance are the white-nosed DVIIs from *Jagdstaffel 12*,
whilst in the far distance can be seen the aircraft of *Jagdstaffel 13*.
Although the full establishment of a *Jagdgeschwader* exceeded fifty
machines, this figure was seldom reached in the last few months of
the war.
106. *Jagdstaffel 36* was the component unit in *Jagdgeschwader III*
destined to receive the Fokker EV, one of which is seen here
marked with the blue nose cowling unit marking; the fuselage band
with star is the pilot's own marking. *Jasta 36* pilots who flew the

parasols considered them *blendend* (dazzling, or brilliant) – praise
indeed from pilots used to such machines as the outstanding Fokker
DVII powered by the BMW engine.
107. Investigation revealed that the shortcomings in the EV's wing
were due to incorrect assembly of the box-spar booms, coupled with
poor gluing and nailing procedures. New wings, incorporating some
modifications, were manufactured under stricter supervision and
the parasol emerged again, designated Fokker DVIII. A few
reached the Front in October 1918 but saw little action in the
closing days of the war. The DVIII shown is 257/18, which was
powered by the 110hp UrII although many aircraft of this type now
used the 160hp UrIII (which was probably less sensitive to the poor
quality *ersatz* lubricating oil then in use).

▼107

108▲

108. Only a small number of Fokker EV/DVIIIs survived to fly again after the war, some being taken to Italy, Holland and the USA. A few were used by the Polish Air Force: EV 185/18 was one, and this aircraft probably served in the 7th Aviation (*Kosciusako*) Squadron fighting against the Ukrainians in 1919. Since the remainder of the machine is intact, it does not appear that the broken mainplane was the result of a flying accident.

109. A Fokker CI two-seater, showing a copybook application of the Dutch civil aircraft registration as defined by the International Convention for Air Navigation in July 1919. This design originated in Schwerin and was derived from the Fokker DVII, but the aircraft was of increased length and wingspan. Total production is thought to have been less than 100, of which some were delivered to the Dutch Army and Naval air services.

109▼

▲110

110. During 1920 Fokker DVII F7716/18 was flown to Sweden and soon afterwards was sold to the Swedish Air Service; its pilot was Hermann Göring, seen on the left. Note that the machine is unarmed and is marked with the black and white band markings of *Jagdstaffel 26*; from the neatness of the detail lettering the unit markings were probably factory-applied. The aircraft is from one of the final production batches, delivered late in 1918.

111. Fokker delivered twenty Fokker DVII machines to the *Luchtvaartafdeling* (*LVA*, or Dutch Army Air Service) in 1920. Ten aircraft, serialled 250–259, were powered by the Mercedes DIII 160hp engine and the remainder were BMW IIIa-powered. Shown is No. 251, marked with the orange-disc Dutch national marking (which was modified in June 1921 to have superimposed red, white and blue outer sectors, leaving only a small central orange spot). Reflections show the glossy finish of the fabric-covered surfaces on this immaculate example.

112. Over 140 Fokker DVIIs went to the United States after the war, many being used as advanced training aircraft by the US Army Air Service. Here, wearing the insignia of the 1st US Aero Squadron, one of these machines is looped over Mitchell Field by Lieutenant Barksdale in 1920. It has been completely overpainted khaki-brown and has had its crosses repainted (with an incorrect type on the rudder), possibly for air show work.

113. Fokker also delivered twenty DVII Fs, powered by the BMW IIIa engine, to the *Marineluchtvaartdienst* (*MLD*, or Dutch Naval Air service), and four of them are seen here formating on a two-seat Fokker CI. Based at De Kooy and Waalhaven, some of the machines shown served from 1920 until they were phased out in 1937. The two aircraft with the blue fuselage and wing bands are from the *Gevechtsescadrille* (fighter squadron) formed for the aerial defence of Den Helder and Flushing.

▼111

▲114　▼115

114. Nearly the real thing! Frank Clarke as *Leutnant* von Bruen in the nearest Fokker DVII, accompanied by Frank Tomick in the other machine, flies over cloud near Oakland, California, in the summer of 1928 during the filming of Howard Hughes' epic *Hell's Angels*. The dog-fight sequence from this film has never been bettered: it involved fifty aeroplanes, most of them genuine First World War machines, and the way they were reefed around the sky and put into vertical dives was, in the judgement of ex-wartime fliers, exactly the style of flying from 1918.

115. Many European countries other than Holland adopted the Fokker DVII for their air arms after the war, sizeable contingents being used, for example, by Belgium and Switzerland. Shown in Swiss service is No. 631, which is thought to have been an Albatros-built machine. There are differences from the original in cowling details and the two longitudinal stringers fitted to the fuselage, and note the pitot head on the top wing leading edge. This unarmed example is BMW IIIa-powered.

116. A number of Fokker DVII variants were manufactured during the late-1920s, including a batch of two-seaters by Julius Hüffer Flugzeugbau of Münster. Known as Huffer H9s, some of these were operated on aerial advertising duties by the Trumpf chocolate company. The example shown here, owned by Leonard Mannheim of Berlin, was damaged on landing after engaging in a race against a speedboat on Berlin's Templiner Lake. Note the gravity fuel tank in the centre section, the belly tank aft of the undercarriage, and the absence of the usual horn balances on the ailerons,

117. An unlikely setting for a Fokker DrI triplane. During 1938 this machine from the *Deutscheluftfahrtsammlung* (German Aviation Collection) in Berlin was overhauled to flying condition and used in the making of Herbert Maish's film *DIII 88*. It is seen here about to be off-loaded on to the quayside at Bug on the island of Rügen in the Baltic. Note that the cowling over the Oberursel engine is of the open-fronted 'horseshoe' type, as used on earlier Fokker designs.

116▲ 117▼

▲118

118. Another Fokker DrI triplane brought out of the *Deutscheluftfahrtsammlung* museum in Berlin was the Clerget-powered 528/17 seen here during the filming of Karl Ritter's *Pour Le Mérite* in 1938. Initially the museum aircraft were to be used as patterns for replica construction, but it proved easier to use the actual machines, and this misuse of privilege resulted in court action against *Hauptmann* Krupp, the museum curator.

119. After a hectic career which included film work in both *Hell's*

Angels and *Men With Wings*, this Fokker DVII spent some time as a two-seater, was re-engined several times (it is shown here with a Wright-Hispano-Suiza V8) and flew as recently as 1963 when in the Tallmantz Collection. It has now been purchased by Fokker, who have placed it on long-term loan with the Dutch Military Museum in Soesterburg, where it is currently being refurbished by aviation enthusiasts and former Fokker employees.

▼119